Sunshine & Sunflowers... Block of the Month

pieced by Donna Hansen
quilted by Sue Needle

Enjoy this stunning array of beautiful quilt blocks designed to stimulate your imagination and inspire your creativity. Popular scrappy look quilts have a charming emotional appeal that touches the soul as much as it warms the body.

Simply beautiful... this quilt is charming in any color combination. I love this combination of piecing, applique and basic embroidery. Even beginning quilters will love making this beauty, and they will learn a new tip with each block.

The variety of fabrics in a scrappy quilt entices the eye with pattern and color. Endless possibilities for design and drama continue to make 'Block of the Month' quilts a favorite.

Save time with fabric collections.

Fabric 'collections' can often be purchased in bundles of coordinating colors and prints.

Cut fabric with a sharp rotary cutter, a quilter's ruler and a self-healing cutting mat.

Your private stash of assorted fabrics is also a wonderful source for 'scrappy quilts'.

SIZE: 64" x 74"
YARDAGE:
We used *E.E. Schenck Company/Maywood Studio*
Full Sun by WillowBerry Lane
- Dark Blue - 1 Yard
- Black - 1/2 Yard
- Red - 1/2 Yard
- Gold - 1/2 Yard
- Cream - 1/4 Yard
- Green - 1/2 Yard
- Dark Red - 1/6 Yard
- Light Blue - 2/3 Yard

Border #1	Purchase 1/2 yard Cream
Border #2	Purchase 1/4 yard Red
Border #3	Purchase 1/4 yard Dark Blue
Border #4 & Binding	Purchase 1 1/2 yards Black
Backing	Purchase 4 yards
Batting	Purchase 72" x 82"

Sewing machine, needle, thread
DMC Pearl cotton (Leaf Green, Olive Green, Burgundy, Gold)
Chenille needle 22

Fabric is from *E.E. Schenck Company/Maywood Studio*
www.maywoodstudio.com www.eeschenck.com

Sunshine & Sunflowers
10 different Blocks plus the Border

Sunshine & Sunflowers

Block of the Month Quilt

10 different Blocks plus the Border

PREPARATION FOR BLOCKS

Tip: As you cut the pieces, label them for future reference and easy assembly.

Big Sunflower:

Cut 1 Dark Blue background 18½" x 42½".
Cut 19 Gold strips for petals 2½" x 5".
Cut 1 Black square 8½" x 8½" for the flower.
Cut 1 Dark Red square 5" x 5" for flower center.
Cut 4 Green rectangles 3½" x 8½" for leaves.

Fence:

Cut 4 Cream fence posts 2½" x 14½".
Cut 5 Green strips 2½" x 12½".
Cut 9 Dark Blue squares 2½" x 2½".

Sun:

Cut 1 Light Blue background 18½" x 20½".
Cut 1 Gold square 12½" x 12½".

Horizontal Bars:

Cut 5 Gold strips 2½" x 10½".
Cut 4 Light Blue strips 2½" x 6½".
Cut 4 Dark Blue strips 2½" x 7".

Half-Square Triangles:

Cut 4 Red squares 5" x 5".
Cut 4 Cream squares 5" x 5".

House 1:

Cut Red walls: one 2½" x 6½" and
one Red 6½" x 6½.
Cut 1 Red gable 2½" x 12½".
Cut 1 Black door 4½" x 6½" and
1 Black roof 6½" x 12½".
Cut 2 Dark Blue sky squares 6½" x 6½".
Cut 1 Dark Blue sky rectangle 4½" x 12½".

House 2:

Cut Red walls: one 2½" x 8½" and
one Red 6½" x 8½.
Cut 1 Red gable 4½" x 12½".
Cut 1 Black door 4½" x 8½" and
1 Black roof 6½" x 12½".
Cut 2 Dark Blue sky squares 6½" x 6½".

Two-Flowers Block:

Cut 1 Green background 12½" x 14½".
Cut 2 Gold squares for flowers 4½" x 4½".
Cut 4 Red rectangles for leaves 1½" x 3½".

Pinwheel:

Cut 2 Green 7" x 7" squares and
2 Gold 7" x 7" squares.

Checkerboard:

Cut 1 Dark Red and
1 Red strip 2½" x 17½".
Cut 1 Dark Red square 2½" x 2½".

Sashings:

Cut 1 Dark Blue Sash A 2½" x 30½" and
1 Dark Blue Sash E 2½" x 18½".
Cut 1 Black Sash B 2½" x 30½".
Cut 1 Red Sash C 2½" x 18½".
Cut 1 Light Blue Sash D 2½" x 30½" and
1 Light Blue Sash F 2½" x 34½".

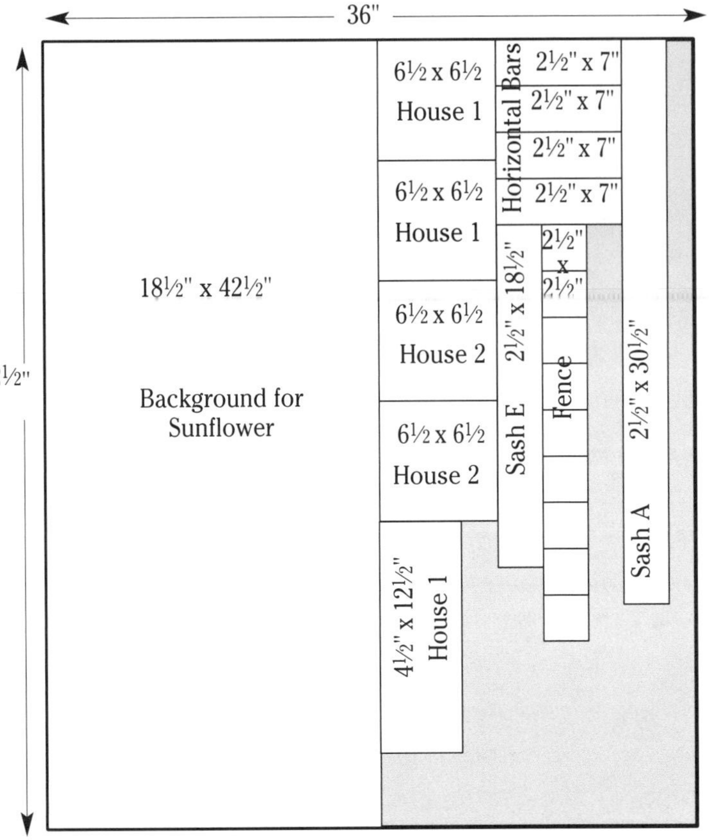

Dark Blue - 1 Yard

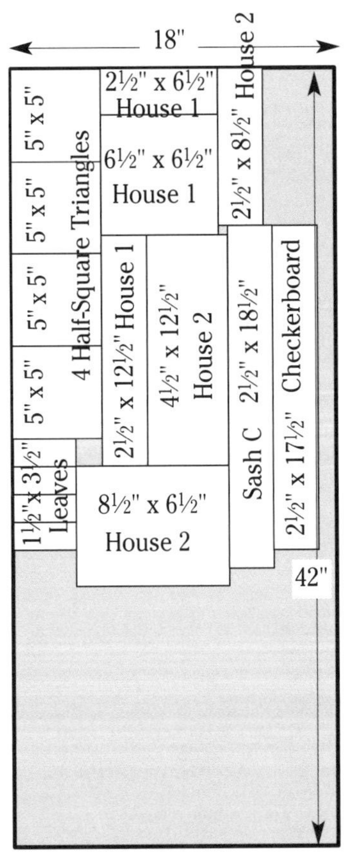

Red - ½ Yard

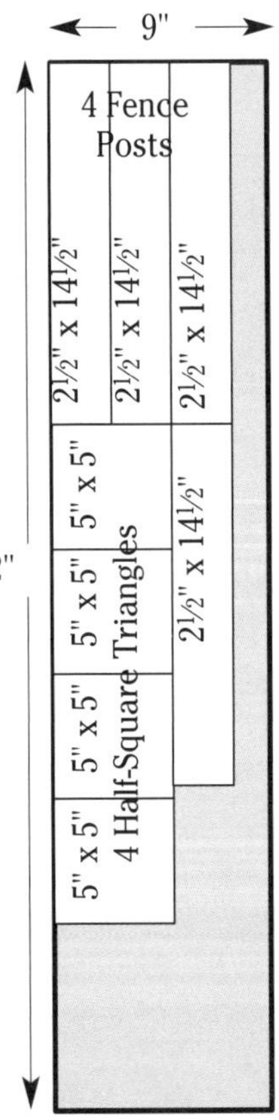

Cream - ¼ Yard

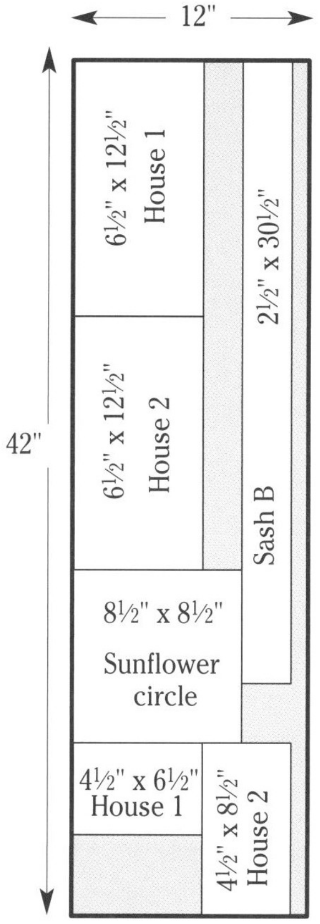

Black - ⅓ Yard

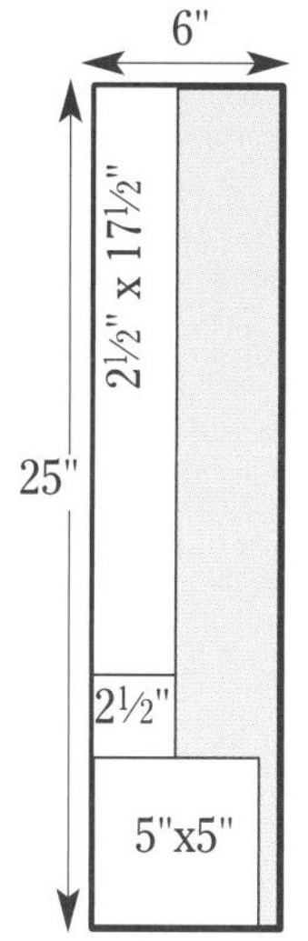

Dark Red - ⅙ Yard

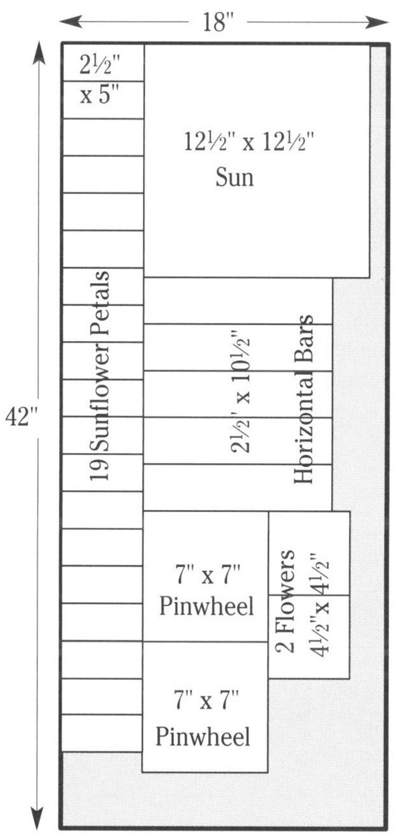

Gold - ½ Yard

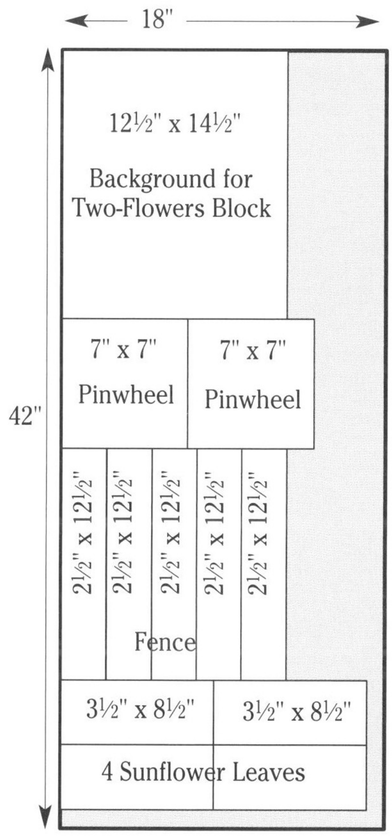

Green - ½ Yard

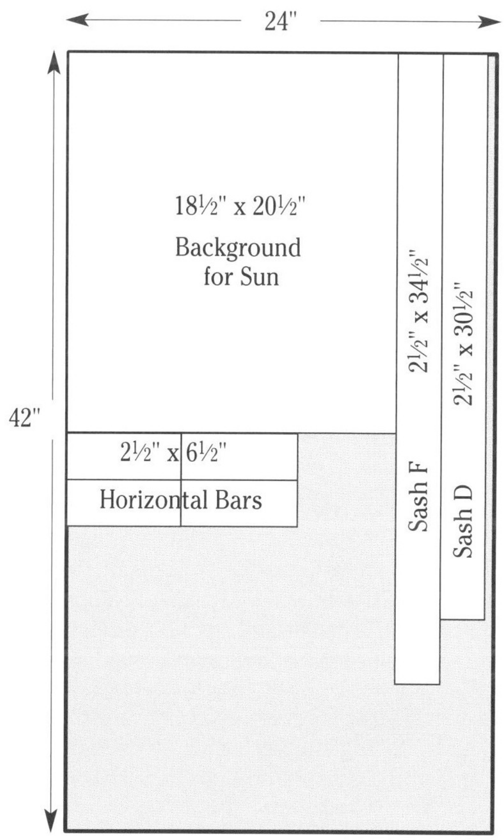

Light Blue - ⅔ Yard

MAKING THE BLOCKS Tip: As you cut the pieces, label them for future reference and easy assembly.

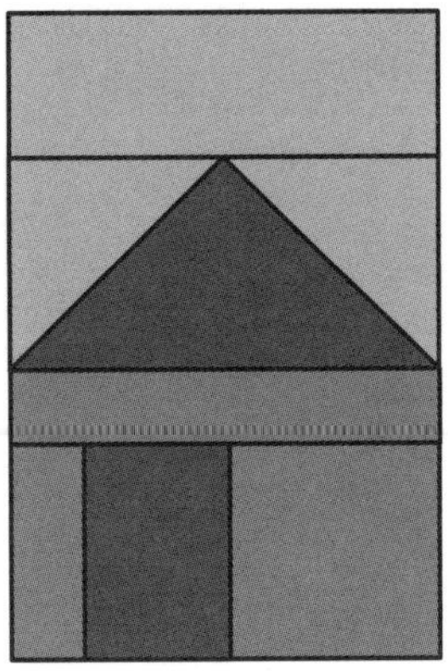

A - House 1 Block

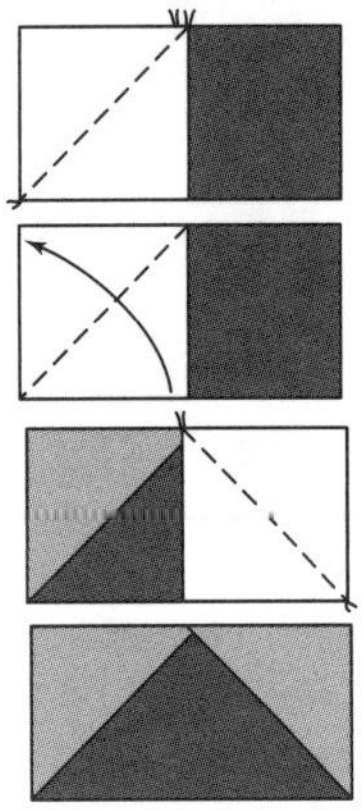

Roof Diagram

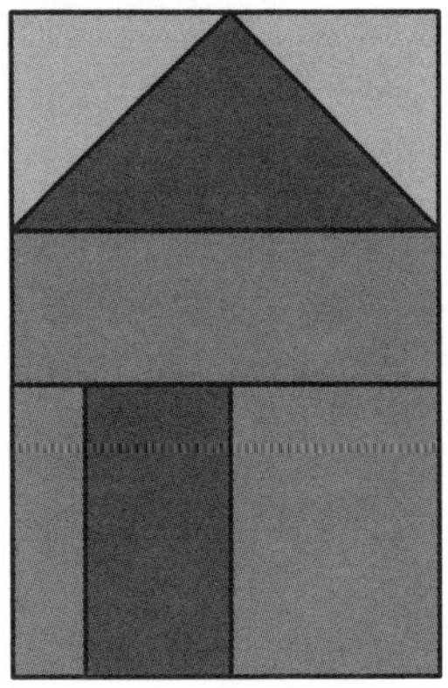

B - House 2 Block

B - House 2:

Wall section:

Sew a Red wall 2½" x 8½" to the door and the other Red 6½" x 8½" wall . Press.

Sew the Red gable 4½" x 12½" to the top of the wall piece.

Roof section:

Follow the instructions for the Roof on House 1.

Assembly:

Sew the roof section to the wall section. Press.

A - House 1:

Wall section:

Sew a Red wall 2½" x 6½" to the door and the other Red 6½" x 6½" wall . Press.

Sew the Red gable 2½" x 12½" to the top of the wall piece.

Roof section:

See the Roof Diagram.

Place the Black roof 6½" x 12½" on the table.

With right sides together, align a Dark Blue sky square with one short edge.

On the wrong side of the Blue square, draw a diagonal from the bottom left to the upper right.

Sew on the diagonal line. Fold back the flap. Press.

Repeat for the other side, drawing the diagonal from the bottom right to the upper left.

Assembly:

Sew the Dark Blue sky rectangle to the top of the roof. Press.

Sew the roof section to the wall section. Press.

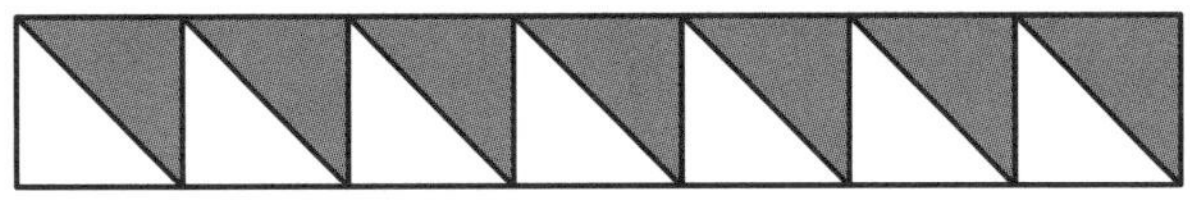

C - Triangles Row

C - Half-Square Triangles Row:

With right sides together, make 4 pairs of Red-Cream squares.

Follow the instructions in the Half-Square Triangle Diagram on page 7.

Align the diagonals as shown in the diagram.

Sew 7 half-square triangles to make a piece 4½" x 28½".

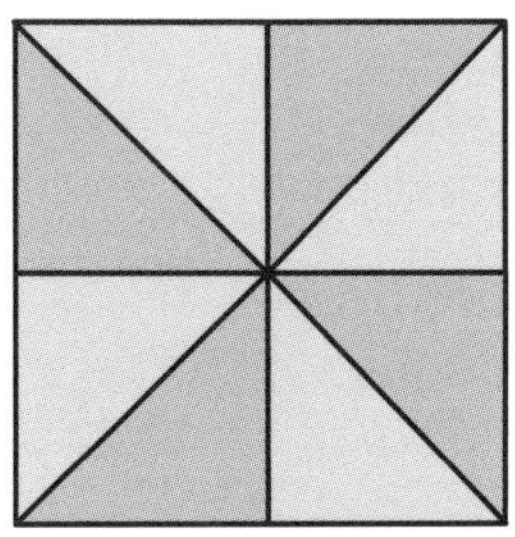

D - Pinwheel Block

D - Pinwheel Block:

With right sides together, make 2 pairs of Green-Gold 7" squares.

Follow the instructions in the Half-Square Pinwheels Triangle Diagram on page 7.

Trim all squares to 6½" x 6½".

Following the Pinwheel diagram, arrange 4 half-square triangles in two rows.

Sew the squares together to form each row. Press.

Sew the rows together. Press.

E - Two-Flowers Block

E - Two-Flowers Block:

Trace each flower onto a Gold 4½" square.

Trace each leaf onto a Red 1½" x 3½" rectangle (see flower and leaf patterns on page 8).

Cut out the flower and leaf shapes leaving a scant ¼" border for turning the edge under.

Embroider the flower centers with Gold and Burgundy Straight stitches.

Sew Running stitches around the edge of the flowers with Gold and around the leaves with Leaf Green.

Embroider the stem with Stem stitches in both shades of Green.

Note: Embroidery Stitch instructions are on page 15.

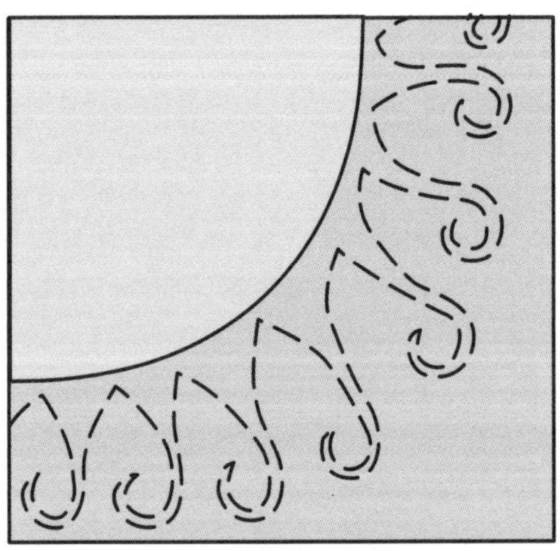

F - Sunshine Block

F - S2unshine Block:

Trace the Sun pattern onto the 12½" Gold square (see sun pattern on pages 12 - 15).

Cut out leaving a scant ¼" border for turning the edge under.

Follow the instructions for Applique on page 11.

Draw the rays of the sun with a blue water soluble marker.

Embroider the rays with Gold Running stitches.

Note: Embroidery Stitches are on page 15.

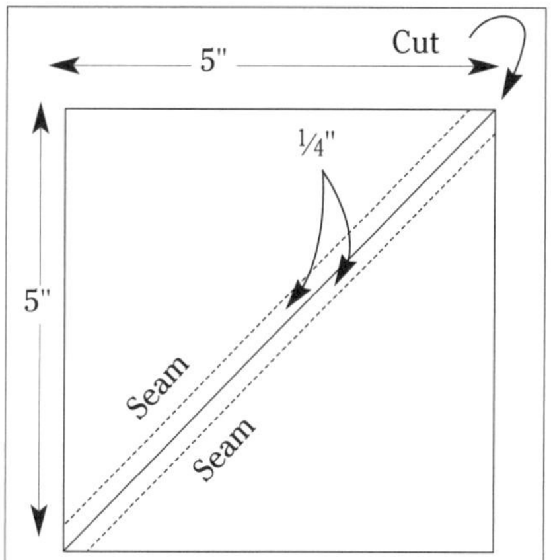

Half-Square Triangle Diagram

1. Place 2 squares right sides together.
2. Draw one diagonal line.
3. Stitch 1/4" on each side of the line.
4. Cut squares apart on the diagonal line.
5. Open the 2 new squares with 2 colors.
6. Press. Trim off dog-ears.
7. Trim to 4½" x 4½".

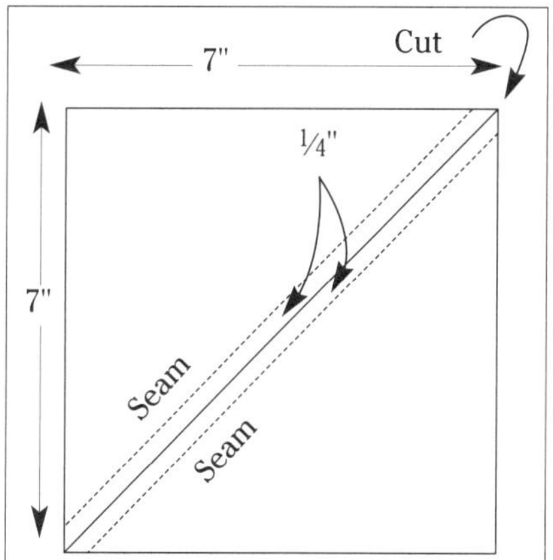

Pinwheels Triangle Diagram

1. Place 2 squares right sides together.
2. Draw one diagonal line.
3. Stitch 1/4" on each side of the line.
4. Cut squares apart on the diagonal line.
5. Open the 2 new squares with 2 colors.
6. Press. Trim off dog-ears.
7. Trim to 6½" x 6½".

G - Big Sunflower Block

G - Big Sunflower:

Draw the petals on the 19 Gold 2½" x 5" strips (Note: Add or subtract petals to fit. See patterns on pages 16 - 17).
Draw the flower circle on the Black 8½" square (see patterns on pages 9 - 10)..
Draw the flower center on the Dark Red 5" square.
Draw a leaf on each Green 3½" x 8½" rectangle.
Cut out all pieces leaving a scant 1/4" border for turning under the edge.
Follow the applique instructions on page 11.
Straight stitch around the Red center with Burgundy, around each leaf with Leaf Green, and around each petal with Gold pearl cotton.
Using Olive pearl cotton, sew 2 rows of Stem stitches about ½" apart. Fill the center with Leaf Green Satin stitches sewn at an angle.

Note: Embroidery Stitches are on page 15.

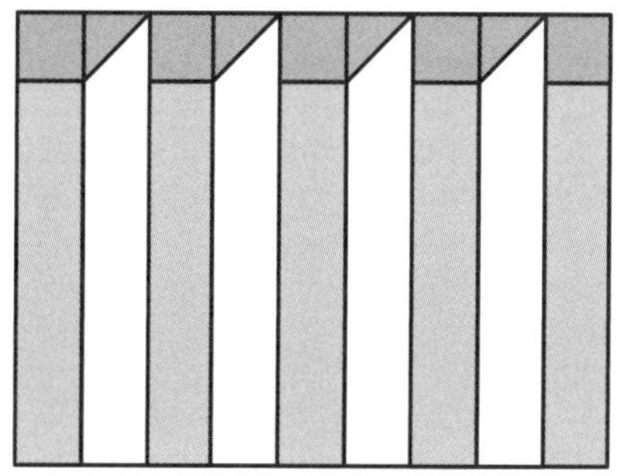

H - Fence Block

H - Fence Block:

Cream Posts:

Place a Cream fence post face up on the table.
With right sides together, align a Dark Blue square at the top of the strip.
Draw a diagonal as shown in the Fence diagram.
Sew on the diagonal. Fold back the flap and press.
Repeat for remaining the 3 Cream posts.

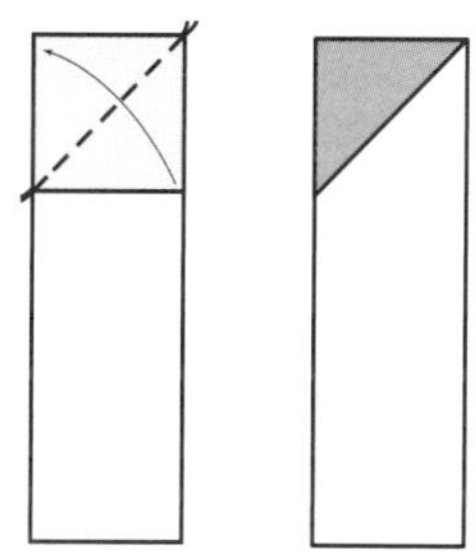

Fence Diagram

Green-Blue strips:

Sew a Dark Blue 2½" square to the top of each Green 2½" x 12½" strip.

Assembly:

Arrange the Green-Blue strips and Cream posts as shown in the Fence Block diagram. Sew the strips together. Press.

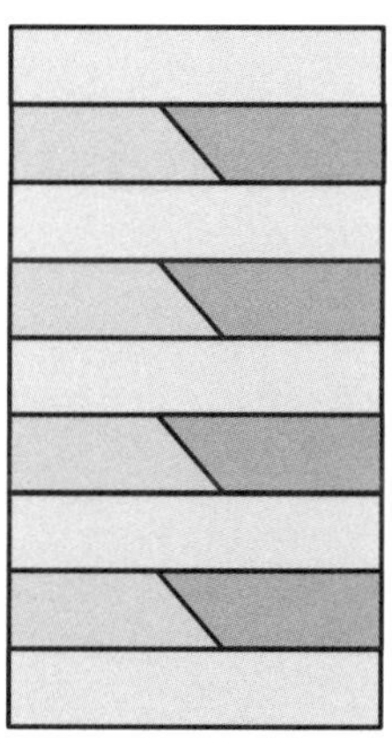

I - Horizontal Bars Block

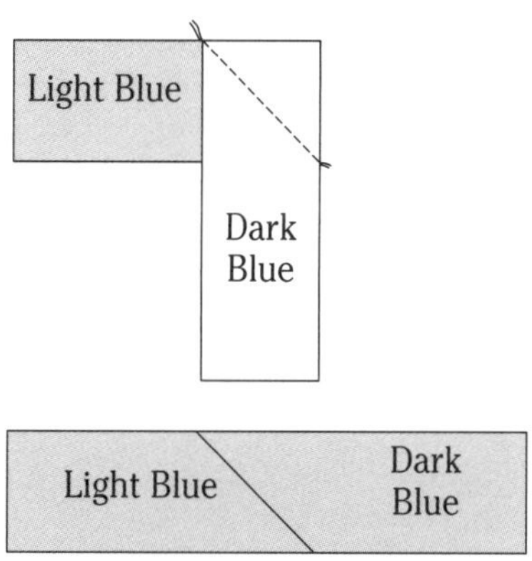

Horizontal Bar Diagram

J - Checkerboard Row

J - Checkerboard:

Sew the Dark Red and Red 2½" x 17½" strips together side by side to make a piece 4½" x 17½". Press.
Cut the piece into 7 strips 4½" long.
Sew the pieces in a line, Dark Red-Red, Dark Red-Red, etc.
Sew 1 Dark Red 2½" square to the end. Press.

I - Horizontal Bars:

Place a Light Blue 2½" x 6½"strip right side up on the table.
With right sides together, position a Dark Blue 2½" x 7" strip as shown in the Horizontal Bar Diagram
Draw a diagonal line as shown and sew on the line.
Fold back the Dark Blue strip and press.

ASSEMBLY:

Lay the blocks and sashing strips on a work surface or table following the diagram.

Sew the Sunshine block F to the Horizontal Bars block I. Press.

Sew Sashing A to the bottom of the piece. Press.

Sew House 1-Sashing E-House 2. Press.

Sew the Two Flowers block E to the Pinwheel block D. Press.

Sew the Two Flowers/Pinwheel piece to the bottom of the Houses to make section A-B-E-D. Press.

Sew Sashing D to the left side of section A-B-E-D. Press.

Sew the Triangles row C to the top of A-B-E-D. Press.

Sew Sashing F to the right side of C-A-B-E-D. Press.

Sew Sashing B and the Checkerboard row J to the bottom. Press.

Sew this piece to the bottom of the Sunshine section to complete the left side of the quilt. Press.

Sew the Big Sunflower block to the Fence block. Press.

Sew Sashing C to the bottom of the fence. Press.

Sew the left and right sections of the quilt together. Press.

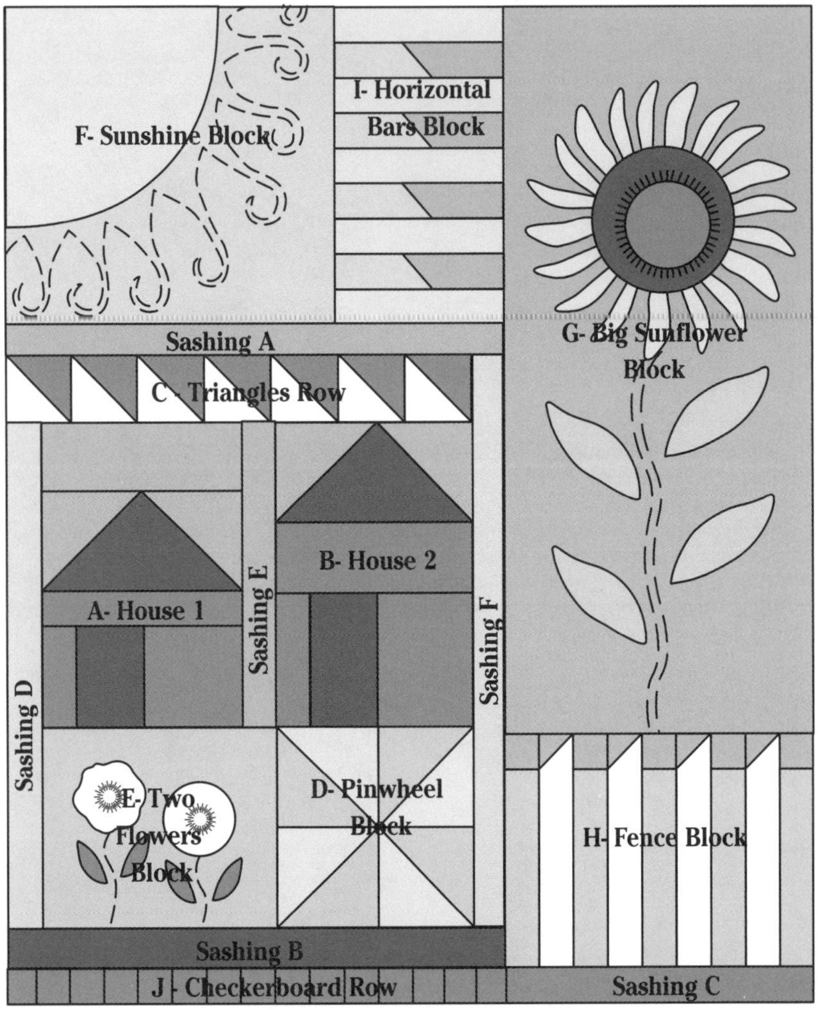

Assembly Diagram

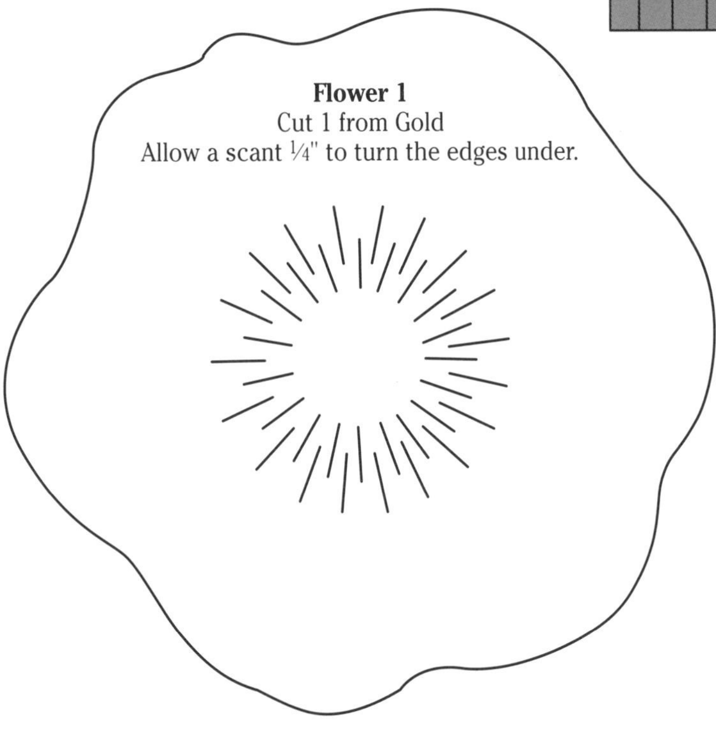

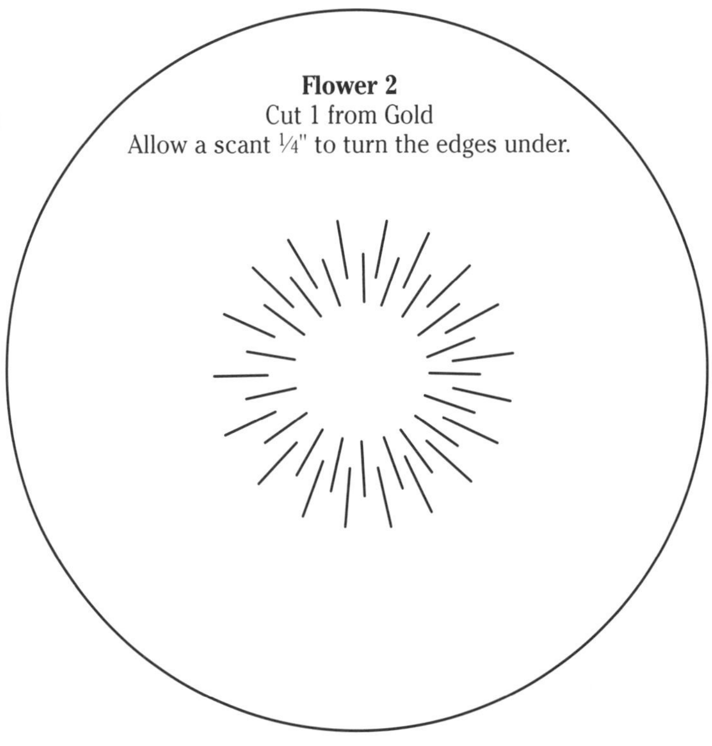

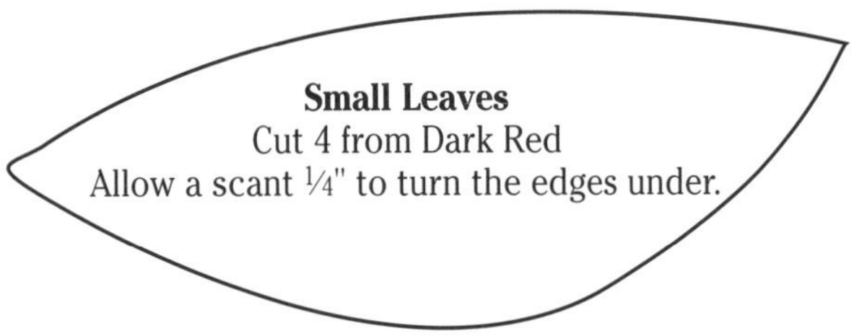

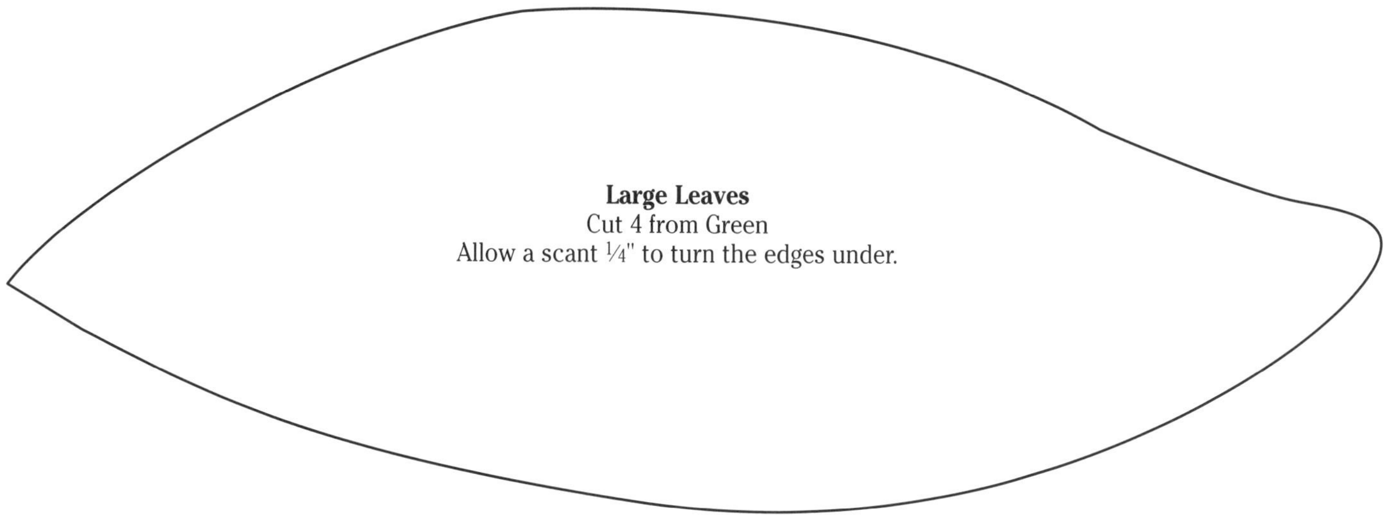

BORDERS:

Cream Border #1:
Cut 2½" strips. Sew strips together end to end.
Cut 2 strips 2½" x 62½" for sides.
Cut 2 strips 2½" x 48½" for top and bottom.
Sew top and bottom borders to the quilt. Press.
Sew side borders to the quilt. Press.

Red Border #2:
Cut 1½" strips. Sew strips together end to end.
Cut 2 strips 1½" x 62½" for sides.
Cut 2 strips 1½" x 54½" for top and bottom.
Sew side borders to the quilt. Press.
Sew top and bottom borders to the quilt. Press.

Dark Blue Border #3:
Cut 1½" strips. Sew strips together end to end.
Cut 2 strips 1½" x 64½" for sides.
Cut 2 strips 1½" x 56½" for top and bottom.
Sew side borders to the quilt. Press.
Sew top and bottom borders to the quilt. Press.

Black Outer Border #4:
Cut 4½" strips. Sew strips together end to end.
Cut 2 strips 4½" x 66½" for sides.
Cut 2 strips 4½" x 64½" for top and bottom.
Sew side borders to the quilt. Press.
Sew top and bottom borders to the quilt. Press.

FINISHING:

Quilting: See Basic Instructions on page 14.

Binding: Cut seven 2½" strips.
Sew together end to end to equal 284".
See Binding Instructions on page 15.

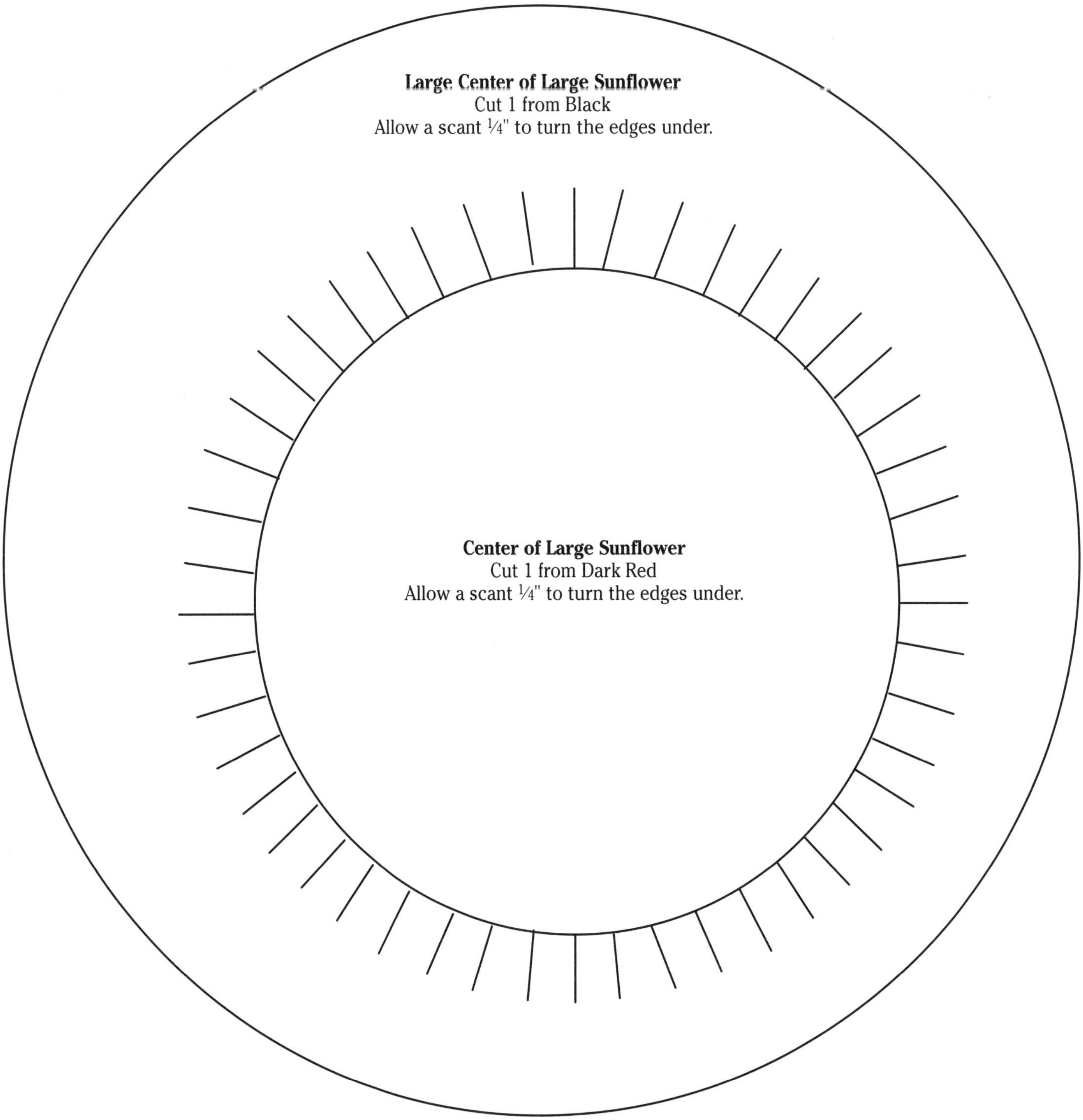
Large Center of Large Sunflower
Cut 1 from Black
Allow a scant 1/4" to turn the edges under.
Center of Large Sunflower
Cut 1 from Dark Red
Allow a scant 1/4" to turn the edges under.

Tips for Strips

TIPS: As a Guide for Yardage:
Each 1/4 yard or a 'Fat Quarter' equals 3 strips
A pre-cut 'Jelly Roll' strip is 2½" x 44"
Cut 'Fat Quarter' strips to 2½" x 22"

Pre-cut strips are cut on the crosswise grain and are prone to stretching. These tips will help reduce stretching and make your quilt lay flat for quilting.

1. If you are cutting yardage, cut on the grain. Cut fat quarters on grain, parallel to the 18" side.

2. When sewing crosswise grain strips together, take care not to stretch the strips. If you detect any puckering as you go, rip out the seam and sew it again.

3. Press, Do Not Iron. Carefully open fabric, with the seam to one side, press without moving the iron. A back-and-forth ironing motion stretches the fabric.

4. Reduce the wiggle in your borders with this technique from garment making. First, accurately cut your borders to the exact measure of the quilt top. Then, before sewing the border to the quilt, run a double row of stay stitches along the outside edge to maintain the original shape and prevent stretching. Pin the border to the quilt, taking care not to stretch the quilt top to make it fit. Pinning reduces slipping and stretching.

Applique Instructions

Basic Turned Edge:
1. Trace pattern onto template plastic.
2. Cut out the shape leaving a scant ¼" fabric border all around and clip the curves.
3. Place the template plastic on the wrong side of the fabric. Spray edges with starch.
4. Press the ⅛" border over the edge of the template plastic with the tip of a hot iron. Press firmly.
5. Remove the template, maintaining the folded edge on the back of the fabric.
6. Position the shape on the quilt and Blindstitch in place.

Basic Needle Turn:
1. Cut out the shape leaving a ¼" fabric border all around.
2. Baste the shapes to the quilt, keeping the basting stitches away from the edge of the fabric.
3. Begin with all areas that are under other layers and work to the topmost layer.
4. For an area no more than 2" ahead of where you are working, trim to ⅛" and clip the curves.
5. Using the needle, roll the edge under and sew tiny Blindstitches to secure.

Using Fusible Web for Iron-on Applique:
1. Trace the pattern onto *Steam a Seam 2* fusible web.
2. Press the patterns onto the wrong side of the fabric.
3. Cut out patterns exactly on the drawn line.
4. Score the web paper with a pin, then remove the paper.
5. Position the fabric, fusible side down, on the quilt. Press with a hot iron following the fusible web manufacturer's instructions.
6. Stitch around the edge by hand.

Optional: Stabilize the wrong side of the fabric with your favorite stabilizer.

Use a size 80 machine embroidery needle. Fill the bobbin with lightweight basting thread and thread the machine with a machine embroidery thread that complements the color being appliqued.

Set your machine for a Zigzag stitch and adjust the thread tension if needed. Use a scrap to experiment with different stitch widths and lengths until you find the one you like best.

Sew slowly.

Basic Cutting Instructions

Tips for Accurate Cutting:

Accurate cutting is easy when using a rotary cutter with a sharp blade, a cutting mat, and a transparent ruler. Begin by pressing your fabric and then follow these steps:

1. Folding:

a) Fold the fabric with the selvage edges together. Smooth the fabric flat. If needed, fold again to make your fabric length smaller than the length of the ruler.

b) Align the fold with one of the guide lines on the mat. This is important to avoid getting a kink in your strip.

2. Cutting:

a) Align the ruler with a guide line on the mat. Press down on the ruler to prevent it shifting or have someone help hold the ruler. Hold the rotary cutter along the edge of the ruler and cut off the selvage edge.

b) Also using the guide line on the mat, cut the ends straight.

c) Strips for making the quilt top may be cut on 'crosswise grain' (from selvage to selvage) or 'on grain' (parallel to the selvage edge).

Strips for borders should be cut on grain (parallel to the selvage edge) to prevent wavy edges and make quilting easier.

d) When cutting strips, move the ruler, NOT the fabric.

Rotary Cutting Tips

Rotary Cutter: Friend or Foe

A rotary cutter is a wonderful and useful. When not used correctly, the sharp blade can be a dangerous tool. Follow these safety tips:
1. Never cut toward you.
2. Use a sharp blade. Pressing harder on a dull blade can cause the blade to jump the ruler and injure your fingers.
3. Always disengage the blade before the cutter leaves your hand, even if you intend to pick it up immediately.

Rotary cutters have been caught when lifting fabric, have fallen onto the floor and have cut fingers.

Basic Sewing Instructions

You now have precisely cut strips that are exactly the correct width. You are well on your way to blocks that fit together perfectly. Accurate sewing is the next important step.

Matching Edges:

1. Carefully line up the edges of your strips. Many times, if the underside is off a little, your seam will be off by 1/8". This does not sound like much until you have 8 seams in a block, each off by 1/8". Now your finished block is a whole inch wrong!

2. Pin the pieces together to prevent them shifting.

Seam Allowance:

I cannot stress enough the importance of accurate 1/4" seams. All the quilts in this book are measured for 1/4" seams unless otherwise indicated.

Most sewing machine manufacturers offer a Quarter-inch foot. A Quarter-inch foot is the most worthwhile investment you can make in your quilting.

Pressing:

I want to talk about pressing even before we get to sewing because proper pressing can make the difference between a quilt that wins a ribbon at the quilt show and one that does not.

Press, do NOT iron. What does that mean? Many of us want to move the iron back and forth along the seam. This "ironing" stretches the strip out of shape and creates errors that accumulate as the quilt is constructed. Believe it or not, there is a correct way to press your seams, and here it is:

1. Do NOT use steam with your iron. If you need a little water, spritz it on.

2. Place your fabric flat on the ironing board without opening the seam. Set a hot iron on the seam and count to 3. Lift the iron and move to the next position along the seam. Repeat until the entire seam is pressed. This sets and sinks the threads into the fabric.

3. Now, carefully lift the top strip and fold it away from you so the seam is on one side. Usually the seam is pressed toward the darker fabric, but often the direction of the seam is determined by the piecing requirements.

4. Press the seam open with your fingers. Add a little water or spray starch if it wants to close again. Lift the iron and place it on the seam. Count to 3. Lift the iron again and continue until the seam is pressed. Do NOT use the tip of the iron to push the seam open. So many people do this and wonder later why their blocks are not fitting together.

5. Most critical of all: For accuracy every seam must be pressed before the next seam is sewn.

Working with 'Crosswise Grain' strips:

Strips cut on the crosswise grain (from selvage to selvage) have problems similar to bias edges and are prone to stretching. To reduce stretching and make your quilt lay flat for quilting, keep these tips in mind.

1. Take care not to stretch the strips as you sew.

2. Adjust the sewing thread tension and the presser foot pressure if needed.

3. If you detect any puckering as you go, rip out the seam and sew it again. It is much easier to take out a seam now than to do it after the block is sewn.

Sewing Bias Edges:

Bias edges wiggle and stretch out of shape very easily. They are not recommended for beginners, but even a novice can accomplish bias edges if these techniques are employed.

1. Stabilize the bias edge with one of these methods:

a) Press with spray starch.

b) Press freezer paper or removable iron-on stabilizer to the back of the fabric.

c) Sew a double row of stay stitches along the bias edge and 1/8" from the bias edge. This is a favorite technique of garment makers.

2. Pin, pin, pin! I know many of us dislike pinning, but when working with bias edges, pinning makes the difference between intersections that match and those that do not.

Building Better Borders:

Wiggly borders make a quilt very difficult to finish. However, wiggly borders can be avoided with these techniques.

1. Cut the borders on grain. That means cutting your strips parallel to the selvage edge.

2. Accurately cut your borders to the exact measure of the quilt.

3. If your borders are piece stripped from crosswise grain fabrics, press well with spray starch and sew a double row of stay stitches along the outside edge to maintain the original shape and prevent stretching.

4. Pin the border to the quilt, taking care not to stretch the quilt top to make it fit. Pinning reduces slipping and stretching.

Basic Layering Instructions

Marking Your Quilt:

If you choose to mark your quilt for hand or machine quilting, it is much easier to do so before layering. Press your quilt before you begin. Here are some handy tips regarding marking.

1. A disappearing pen may vanish before you finish.
2. Use a White pencil on dark fabrics.
3. If using a washable Blue pen, remember that pressing may make the pen permanent.

Pieced Backings:

1. Press the backing fabric before measuring.
2. If possible cut backing fabrics on grain, parallel to the selvage edges.
3. Piece 3 parts rather than 2 whenever possible, sewing 2 side borders to the center. This reduces stress on the pieced seam.
4. The backing and batting should extend at least 2" on each side of the quilt.

Creating a Quilt Sandwich:

1. Press the backing and top to remove all wrinkles.
2. Lay the backing wrong side up on the table.
3. Position the batting over the backing and smooth out all wrinkles.
4. Center the quilt top over the batting leaving a 2" border all around.
5. Pin the layers together with 2" safety pins positioned a handwidth apart. A grapefruit spoon makes inserting the pins easier. Leaving the pins open in the container speeds up the basting on the next quilt.

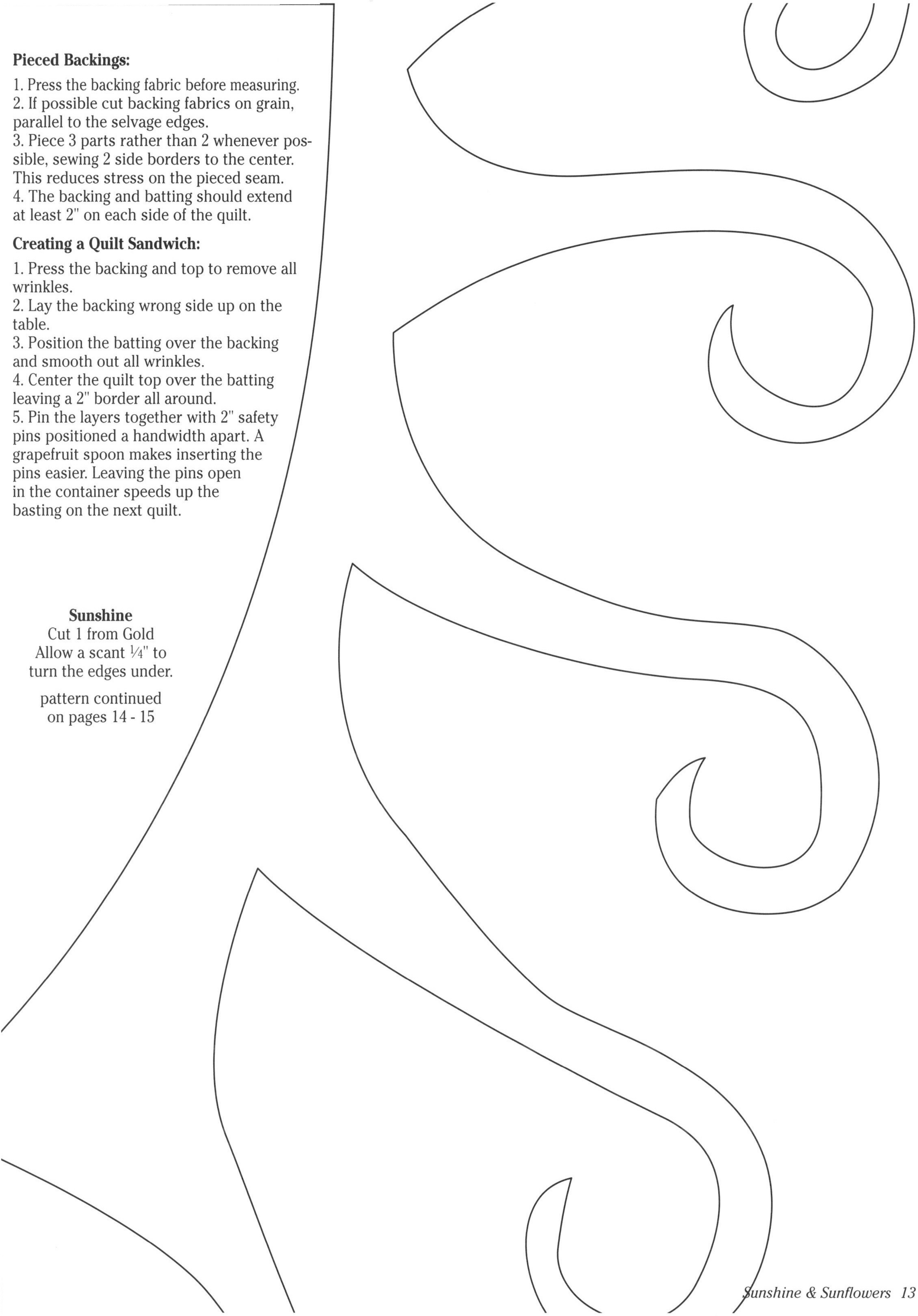

Sunshine
Cut 1 from Gold
Allow a scant $\frac{1}{4}$" to turn the edges under.

pattern continued on pages 14 - 15

Sunshine

pattern continued from pages 12 - 13

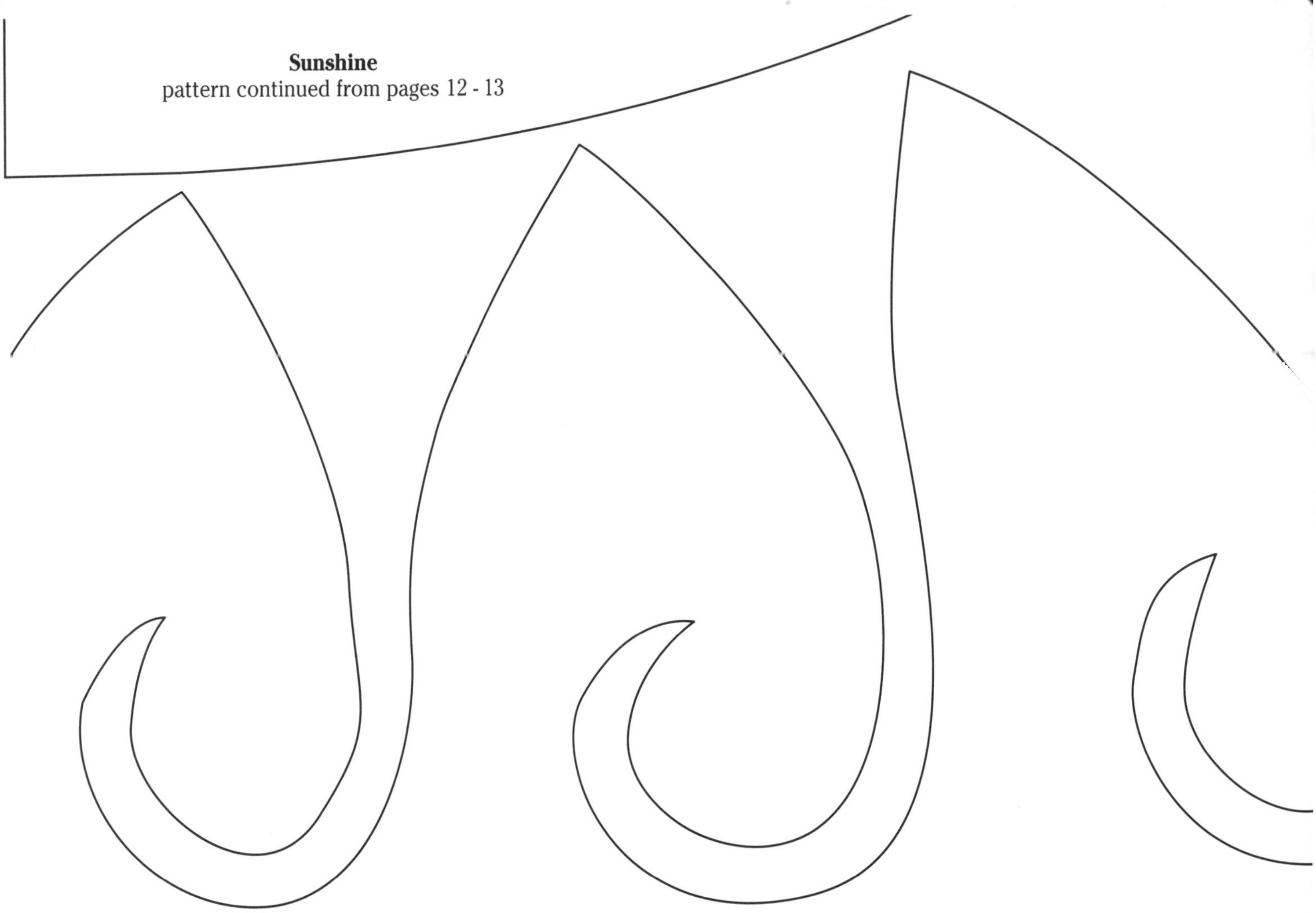

Basic Quilting Instructions

Hand Quilting:

Many quilters enjoy the serenity of hand quilting. Because the quilt is handled a great deal, it is important to securely baste the sandwich together. Place the quilt in a hoop and don't forget to hide your knots.

Machine Quilting:

All the quilts in this book were machine quilted. Some were quilted on a large, free-arm quilting machine and others were quilted on a sewing machine. If you have never machine quilted before, practice on some scraps first.

Straight Line Machine Quilting Tips:

1. Pin baste the layers securely.

2. Set up your sewing machine with a size 80 quilting needle and a walking foot.

3. Experimenting with the decorative stitches on your machine adds interest to your quilt. You do not have to quilt the entire piece with the same stitch. Variety is the spice of life, so have fun trying out stitches you have never used before as well as your favorite stand-bys.

Free Motion Machine Quilting Tips:

1. Pin baste the layers securely.

2. Set up your sewing machine with a spring needle, a quilting foot, and lower the feed dogs.

Basic Mitered Binding Instructions

A Perfect Finish:

The binding endures the most stress on a quilt and is usually the first thing to wear out. For this reason, we recommend using a double fold binding.

1. Trim the backing and batting even with the quilt edge.

2. If possible cut strips on the crosswise grain because a little bias in the binding is a Good thing. This is the only place in the quilt where bias is helpful, for it allows the binding to give as it is turned to the back and sewn in place.

3. Strips are usually cut 2½" wide, but check the instructions for your project before cutting.

4. Sew strips end to end to make a long strip sufficient to go all around the quilt plus 4" - 6".

5. With wrong sides together, fold the strip in half lengthwise. Press.

6. Stretch out your hand and place your little finger at the corner of the quilt top. Place the binding where your thumb touches the edge of the quilt. Aligning the edge of the quilt with the raw edges of the binding, pin the binding in place along the first side.

7. Leaving a 2" tail for later use, begin sewing the binding to the quilt with a ¼" seam.

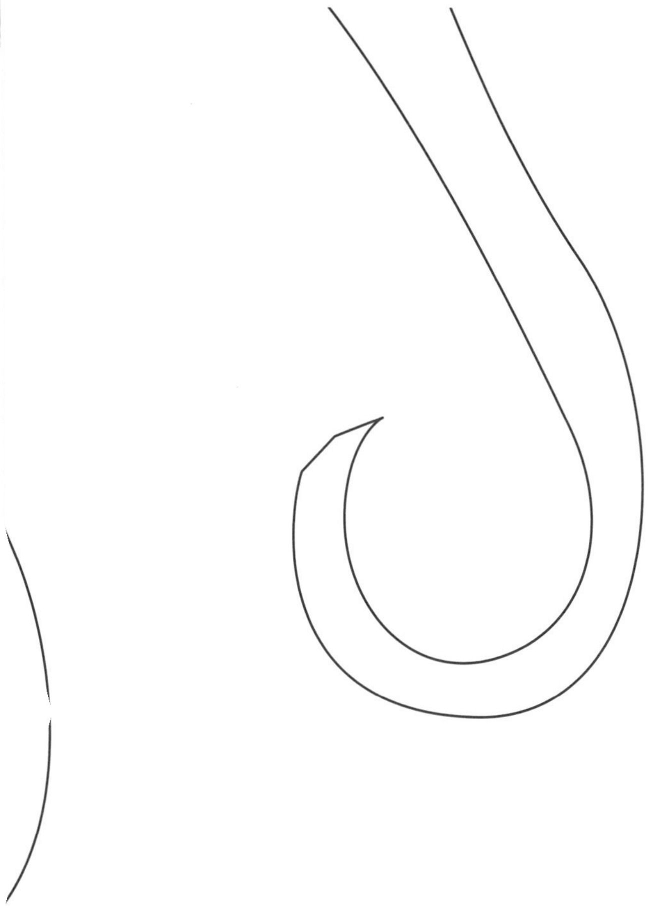

Embroidery

Working with Floss. Use 24" lengths of 6-ply floss and a #22 Chenille needle (this needle has a large eye). Outline large elements of the design with a Running stitch and embroidery patterns.

Running Stitch

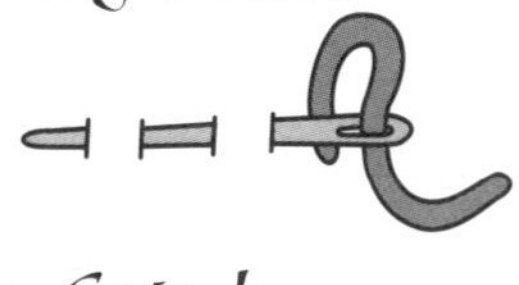

Come up at A. Weave the needle through the fabric, making short, even stitches. Use this stitch to gather fabrics, too.

Satin Stitch

Work small straight stitches close together and at the same angle to fill an area with stitches. Vary the length of the stitches as required to keep the outline of the area smooth.

Stem Stitch

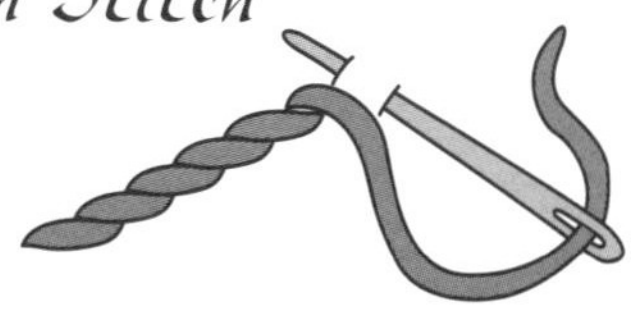

Work from left to right to make regular, slanting stitches along the stitch line. Bring the needle up above the center of the last stitch. Also called 'Outline' stitch.

Straight Stitch

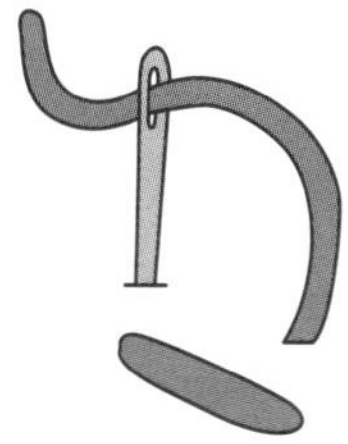

Come up at A and go down at B to form a simple flat stitch. Use this stitch for hair for animals, for simple petals on small flowers and for flower centers.

For Mitered Corners:

1. Stop ¼" from the first corner. Leave the needle in the quilt and turn it 90°. Hit the reverse button on your machine and back off the quilt leaving the threads connected.
2. Fold the binding perpendicular to the side you sewed, making a 45° angle. Carefully maintaining the first fold, bring the binding back along the edge to be sewn.
3. Carefully align the edges of the binding with the quilt edge and sew as you did the first side. Repeat this process until you reach the tail left at the beginning. Fold the tail out of the way and sew until you are ¼" from the beginning stitches.
4. Remove the quilt from the machine. Fold the quilt out of the way and match the binding tails together. Carefully sew the binding tails with a ¼" seam. You can do this by hand if you prefer.

Finishing the Binding:

5. Trim the seam to reduce bulk.
6. Finish stitching the binding to the quilt across the join you just sewed.
7. Turn the binding to the back of the quilt. To reduce bulk at the corners, fold the miter in the opposite direction from which it was folded on the front.
8. Hand-sew a Blind stitch on the back of the quilt to secure the binding in place.

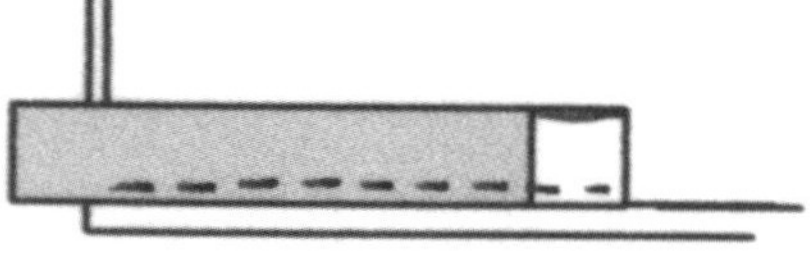

Align the raw edge of the binding with the raw edge of the quilt top. Start about 8" from the corner and go along the first side with a ¼" seam.

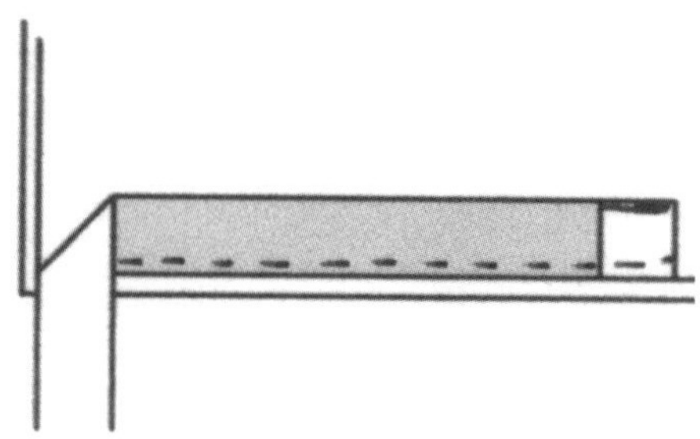

Stop ¼" from the edge. Then stitch a slant to the corner (through both layers of binding)... lift up, then down, as you line up the edge. Fold the binding back.

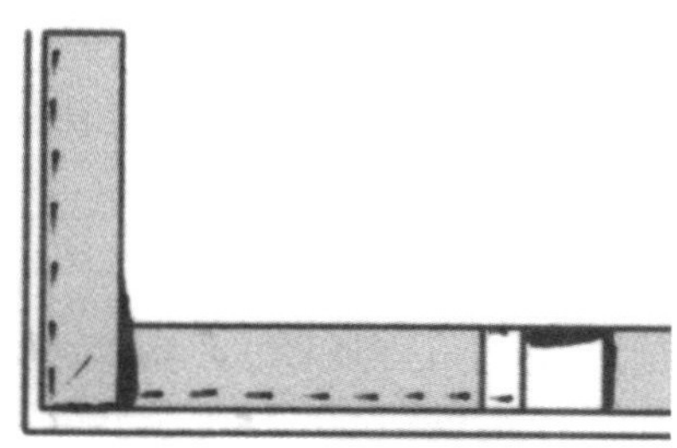

Align the raw edge again. Continue stitching the next side with a ¼" seam as you sew the binding in place.

Sunflowers

Optional Design -
6 Blocks
3 Sunflowers & Fence

SIZE: 70" x 72"

YARDAGE:

We used Full Sun from Maywood Studio

- Dark Blue - 1¾ Yards
- Black - ¼ Yard
- Gold - ½ Yard
- Green - ⅝ Yard
- Cream - ½ Yard

Border #1	Purchase ½ yard Cream
Border #2 & flower center	Purchase ½ yard Red
Border #3	Purchase ¼ yard Dark Blue
Border #4 & Binding	Purchase 1⅜ yards Black
Backing	Purchase 4¼ yards
Batting	Purchase 78" x 80"

Sewing machine, needle, thread

DMC Pearl cotton (Grass Green, Olive Green, Burgundy, Gold)

PREPARATION FOR BLOCKS

G - Big Sunflower:

Cut 3 Dark Blue backgrounds 18½" x 42½".
Cut 57 Gold strips for petals 2½" x 4½".
Cut 3 Black squares 8½" x 8½" for the flower.
Cut 3 Red square 5" x 5" for flower center.
Cut 12 Green rectangles 3½" x 8½" for leaves.

H - Fence:

Cut 13 Cream fence posts 2½" x 14½".
Cut 14 Green strips 2½" x 12½".
Cut 27 Dark Blue squares 2½" x 2½".

MAKE THE BLOCKS:

Follow the instructions for Blocks G & H on page 7.

G - Big Sunflower Block- Make 3.

H - Fence Block:

Make 14 Green strips with a Blue square on top.
Make 13 Cream fence posts. See the Fence post diagram.
Alternating Green and Cream posts, sew the fence block together, beginning and ending with a Green strip. Press.

ASSEMBLY:

Refer to diagram for block placement and direction.
Sew the 3 Sunflower blocks together. Press.
Sew the fence to the bottom of the sunflowers. Press.

Cream Border #1:

Cut and sew 2½" strips together end to end.
Cut 2 strips 2½" x 60½" for sides.
Cut 2 strips 2½" x 54½" for top and bottom.
Sew top and bottom borders to the quilt. Press.
Sew side borders to the quilt. Press.

For remaining borders, sew the side to the quilt, press, sew the top and bottom borders and press.

Red Border #2:

Cut and sew 1½" strips together end to end.
Cut 2 strips 1½" x 60½" for sides.
Cut 2 strips 1½" x 60½" for top and bottom.

Dark Blue Border #3:

Cut and sew 1½" strips together end to end.
Cut 2 strips 1½" x 62½" for sides.
Cut 2 strips 1½" x 62½" for top and bottom.

Black Outer Border #4:

Cut and sew 4½" strips together end to end.
Cut 2 strips 4½" x 64½" for sides.
Cut 2 strips 4½" x 70½" for top and bottom.

FINISHING:

Quilting: See Basic Instructions on page 14.

Binding: Cut seven 2½" strips.
Sew together end to end to equal 292".
See Binding Instructions on page 15.

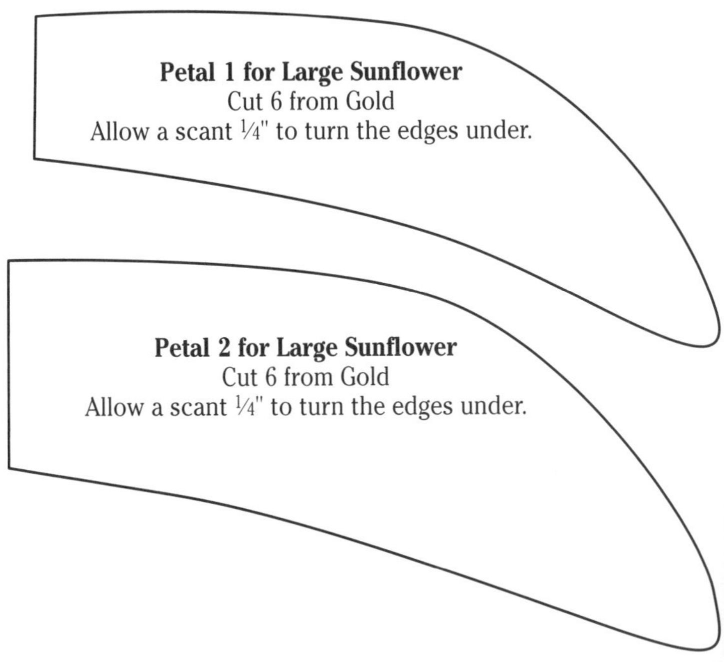

Pinwheels

Optional Design - 9 Blocks
5 Pinwheels & 4 Flowers

SIZE: 52" x 52"
YARDAGE:
We used Full Sun from Maywood Studio
Gold - ⅝ Yard
Green - ¾ Yard

Border #1	Purchase ⅓ yard Cream
Border #2 & leaf appliques	Purchase ¼ yard Red
Border #3	Purchase ⅙ yard Dark Blue
Border #4 & Binding	Purchase 1⅛ yards Black
Backing	Purchase 2½ yards
Batting	Purchase 60" x 60"

Sewing machine, needle, thread
DMC Pearl cotton (Grass Green, Olive Green, Burgundy, Gold)

PREPARATION FOR BLOCKS

D - Pinwheel:
Cut 10 Green and 10 Gold squares 7" x 7".

E - Two-flower Block:
Cut 4 Green backgrounds 12½" x 12½".
Cut 8 Gold squares for flowers 4½" x 4½".
Cut 16 Red rectangles for leaves 1½" x 3½".

MAKE THE BLOCKS:
Follow the instructions for Blocks D & E on page 6.

D - Pinwheel Block - Make 5.

E - Two Flowers Block - Make 4.

ASSEMBLY:
Refer to diagram for block placement and direction.
Sew blocks together in 3 rows, 3 blocks per row. Press.
Sew rows together. Press.

Cream Border #1:
Cut and sew 2½" strips together end to end.
Cut 2 strips 2½" x 40½" for sides.
Cut 2 strips 2½" x 36½" for top and bottom.
Sew top and bottom borders to the quilt. Press.
Sew side borders to the quilt. Press.
For remaining borders, sew the side to the quilt, press, sew the top and bottom borders and press.

Red Border #2:
Cut and sew 1½" strips together end to end.
Cut 2 strips 1½" x 40½" for sides.
Cut 2 strips 1½" x 42½" for top and bottom.

Dark Blue Border #3:
Cut and sew 1½" strips together end to end.
Cut 2 strips 1½" x 42½" for sides.
Cut 2 strips 1½" x 44½" for top and bottom.

Black Outer Border #4:
Cut and sew 4½" strips together end to end.
Cut 2 strips 4½" x 44½" for sides.
Cut 2 strips 4½" x 52½" for top and bottom.

FINISHING:
Quilting: See Basic Instructions on page 14.
Binding: Cut six 2½" strips.
Sew together end to end to equal 216".
See Binding Instructions on page 15.

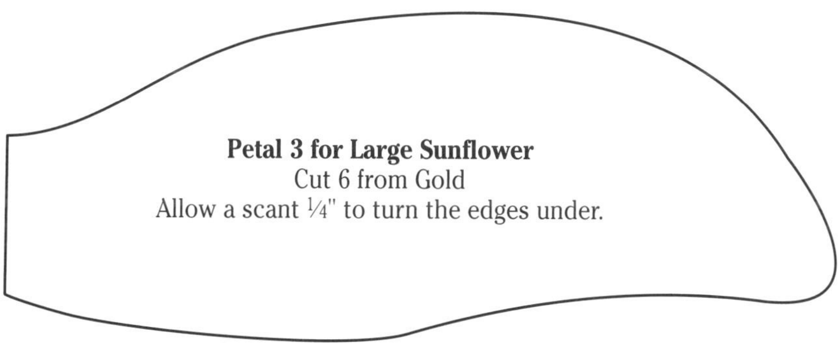

Petal 3 for Large Sunflower
Cut 6 from Gold
Allow a scant ¼" to turn the edges under.

MANY THANKS to my staff for their cheerful help and wonderful ideas!
Kathy Mason • Donna Kinsey
Patty Williams • Janet Long
David & Donna Thomason

Houses

Optional Design
9 Houses & 4 Triangle Rows

Create an attractive quilt by combining colorful house blocks and rows of triangles. This quilt is the perfect size to hang in an entry hall, or to snuggle under when the weather is cool.

SIZE: 60" x 86"
YARDAGE:
We used Full Sun from Maywood Studio
- Red - 1⅓ Yard
- Black - ⅞ Yard
- Light Blue - ¼ Yard
- Dark Blue - 1 Yard
- Cream - ½ Yard

Border #1	Purchase ½ yard Cream
Border #2	Purchase ¼ yard Red
Border #3	Purchase ¼ yard Dark Blue
Border #4 & Binding	Purchase 1⅜ yards Black
Backing	Purchase 4⅓ yards
Batting	Purchase 68" x 94"

Sewing machine, needle, thread

PREPARATION FOR BLOCKS
Tip: As you cut the pieces, label them for future reference and easy assembly.

Half-Square Triangles:
Cut 22 Red and 22 Cream squares 5" x 5".

For 5 of House 1:
Cut Red walls: five 2½" x 6½" and five 6½" x 6½.
Cut 5 Red gables 2½" x 12½".
Cut 5 Black doors 4½" x 6½" and 5 Black roofs 6½" x 12½".
Cut 10 Dark Blue sky squares 6½" x 6½".
Cut 5 Dark Blue sky rectangles 4½" x 12½".

For 4 of House 2:
Cut Red walls: four 2½" x 8½" and four 6½" x 8½.
Cut 4 Red gables 4½" x 12½".
Cut 4 Black doors 4½" x 8½" and 4 Black roofs 6½" x 12½".
Cut 8 Dark Blue sky squares 6½" x 6½".

Sashings:
Cut 6 Dk Blue and 6 Lt. Blue strips 2½" x 18½".

MAKE THE BLOCKS:
Follow the instructions for Blocks A & B on page 6.
A - House 1- Make 5.
B - House 2- Make 4.
C - Triangles row-Make 4 rows:
Follow the instructions for Half-Square triangles on page 7.
Make 44 Red-Cream half-square triangles.
See the diagram for direction of the diagonal and color placement.
Sew 11 half-square triangles together to form a row. Press.

ASSEMBLY:
Arrange all pieces on a work surface or table.
Refer to diagram for block placement and direction.
House Rows 1 & 3: Sew a Light Blue sash-House 1-Dark Blue sash-House 2-Light Blue sash-House 1- Dark Blue sash. Press.
House Row 2: Sew a Dark Blue sash-House 2-Light Blue sash-House 1-Dark Blue sash-House 2- Light Blue sash. Press.
Sew a Triangle row above and below Rows 1 and 3. Press.
Sew the rows together. Press.

Cream Border #1:
Cut and sew 2½" strips together end to end.
Cut 2 strips 2½" x 74½" for sides.
Cut 2 strips 2½" x 44½" for top and bottom.
Sew top and bottom borders to the quilt. Press.
Sew side borders to the quilt. Press.
For remaining borders, sew the sides to the quilt, press, sew the top and bottom borders, and press.

Red Border #2:
Cut and sew 1½" strips together end to end.
Cut 2 strips 1½" x 74½" for sides.
Cut 2 strips 1½" x 50½" for top and bottom.

Dark Blue Border #3:
Cut and sew 1½" strips together end to end.
Cut 2 strips 1½" x 76½" for sides.
Cut 2 strips 1½" x 52½" for top and bottom.

Black Outer Border #4:
Cut and sew 4½" strips together end to end.
Cut 2 strips 4½" x 74½" for sides.
Cut 2 strips 4½" x 60½" for top and bottom.

FINISHING:
Quilting: See Basic Instructions on page 14.
Binding: Cut seven 2½" strips.
Sew together end to end to equal 300".
See Binding Instructions on page 15.

Supplier - Most quilt and fabric stores carry an excellent assortment of supplies. If you need something special, ask your local store to contact the following companies.
FABRICS'
Maywood Fabrics and E.E. Schenck, www.maywoodstudio.com, www.eeschenck.com
QUILTER
Sue Needle, 817-589-1168